# Who is Allah?

Allah is the Creator of the world and the Creator of human beings.

Allah is the Unique, Supreme, and the Lord of the Universe.

Allah is so great that He is beyond our thoughts and imaginations.

He is greater than anything that our limited human minds can come up with; He is above everything and is marvelous.

# Allah
# is the Creator of:

## Universe

**The universe consists of Planets, Stars, and Galaxies.**

# Planet

# Planet

The planet is a large natural body that revolves in an orbit around the Sun or around some other star and that is not radiating energy from internal nuclear fusion reactions.

(Britannica Encyclopedia)

**Eight planets orbiting the Sun:**

Mercury, Venus, Earth, Mars, Jupiter, Saturn, Uranus, and Neptune.

# Star

Any massive self-luminous celestial body of gas that shines by radiation derived from its internal energy sources.

(Britannica Encyclopedia)

**The Sun is a star.**

# Galaxy

"The systems of stars that make up the universe. They are so big that they contain billions of stars".

# Allah
# is the Creator of:

## Earth:

- Earth is the planet on which we reside.

- Earth's surface is about 29% of land and 71% is consists of water.

# Allah
# is the Creator of:

## Sun

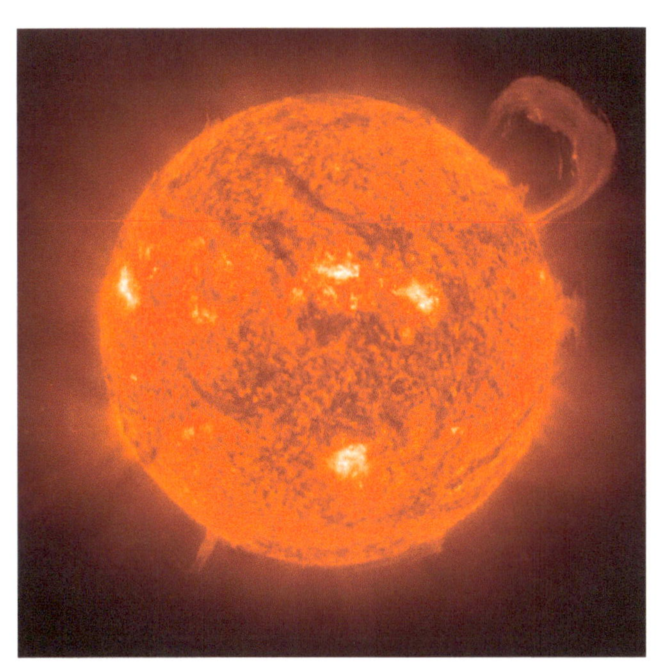

It is an important source of energy for life on Earth.

# Allah
# is the Creator of:

- Mountains
- Trees
- Oceans
- Animals
- Birds

- All these things Worship **Allah**, in a manner that we do not understand.
- The birds, trees, and all other creatures carry out praise of Allah in their own tongue or technique, which completely defies our knowledge.
- But Allah, the most exalted, is well acquainted with their methods.

The Holy Quran specifically declares "the reality of Allah, His inaccessible mystery, His various names, in the 2nd, 59th and 112th chapters of the Quran.

# Quran: Surah 2 (Al – Baqara)

## Verse 255 (Ayatul Kursi)

The Ayat al kursi (Throne Verse) states that nothing and nobody is regarded to be comparable to Allah.

بِسْمِ اللّٰهِ الرَّحْمٰنِ الرَّحِيْمِ

اَللّٰهُ لَآ اِلٰهَ اِلَّا هُوَۚ اَلْحَیُّ الْقَیُّوْمُ

**There is no god except Allah, He is Alive and Eternal.**

The **Alive**, the **Eternal** means that Allah is Self Existing, nothing created him. Allah will never die and He sustains everyone and everything.

**Neither slumber nor sleep overtakes Him.**

Allah is free from all states of drowsiness or sleep. He could never be unaware in regards to His creation. He is Aware of what every soul earns. He never sleeps.

لَهٗ مَا فِی السَّمٰوٰتِ وَمَا فِی الْاَرْضِ ؕ

**Whatsoever is in the heavens and in the earth belongs to Him.**

Allah owned everything on earth or in the heavens. He has the Ultimate Authority.

مَنْ ذَا الَّذِىْ يَشْفَعُ عِنْدَهٗۤ اِلَّا بِاِذْنِهٖ

**Who is he that intervenes with Him except by His authority?**

يَعْلَمُ مَا بَيْنَ أَيْدِيهِمْ وَمَا خَلْفَهُمْ ۖ

**He knows that which is in front of them and that, which is behind them,**

This states His Perfect Knowledge of all creations including the past, present, and future. This is proof of Allah's Knowledge that encompasses all the worlds.

وَلَا يُحِيطُونَ بِشَيْءٍ مِّنْ عِلْمِهِۦٓ إِلَّا بِمَا شَآءَ

**they encompass nothing of His Knowledge except what He will.**

No one attains any knowledge except that which Allah allows.

وَسِعَ كُرۡسِيُّهُ ٱلسَّمَٰوَٰتِ وَٱلۡأَرۡضَۖ

**His throne includes the heavens and the earth,**

The word Kursi represents the Throne of Allah. Allah's Existence, Sovereignty, Power, and Knowledge extend over the heavens and the earth.

**And He is never weary of preserving them.**

Allah has no trouble in managing whatever is in the heavens and the earth. This is an easy matter for Him.

**He is the Magnificent, the Tremendous.**

Allah is the Most Exalted and the Greatest. All honors, power, and superiority belong to none but Allah. He is the Highest, the Greatest.

# Quran: Surah 59 (Al – Hashr) Verse 22 - 24

بِسۡمِ اللّٰهِ الرَّحۡمٰنِ الرَّحِيۡمِ

هُوَ اللّٰهُ الَّذِىۡ لَاۤ اِلٰهَ اِلَّا هُوَ ۚ

عٰلِمُ الۡغَيۡبِ وَالشَّهَادَةِ ۚ هُوَ الرَّحۡمٰنُ الرَّحِيۡمُ

**Allah is He, than Whom there is no other god; He knows all things both secret and open. He is Most Gracious, Most Merciful.**

هُوَ اللّٰهُ الَّذِىْ لَآ اِلٰهَ اِلَّا هُوَ ۚ اَلْمَلِكُ الْقُدُّوْسُ

السَّلٰمُ الْمُؤْمِنُ الْمُهَيْمِنُ الْعَزِيْزُ الْجَبَّارُ الْمُتَكَبِّرُ ؕ

سُبْحٰنَ اللّٰهِ عَمَّا يُشْرِكُوْنَ

**He is Allah, Whom there is no other god; the Sovereign, the Holy One, the Source of Peace, the Guardian of Faith, the Preserver of Safety, the Exalted in Might, the Irresistible, the Supreme: Glory to Allah. He is High above the partners they attribute to Him.**

# هُوَ اللّٰهُ الْخَالِقُ

الْبَارِئُ الْمُصَوِّرُ لَهُ الْاَسْمَآءُ الْحُسْنٰى ۭ يُسَبِّحُ لَهٗ مَا

فِي السَّمٰوٰتِ وَالْاَرْضِ ۚ وَهُوَ الْعَزِيْزُ الْحَكِيْمُ

Allah, He is the Creator, the Evolver, the Bestower of Forms. To Him belongs the Most Beautiful Names: whatever is in the heavens and on earth, declare His Praises and Glory and He is the Glorious in Might, the Wise.

## Quran: Surah 112 (Al-Ikhlas) (Purity)

**The Reason for the Revelation of this Surah and its Virtues:**

Imam Ahmad recorded from Ubayy bin Kaab that the idolaters said to the Prophet, "O Muhammad (Peace be upon him)! Tell us the lineage of your Lord.'' So Allah revealed that Surah.

بِسۡمِ ٱللَّهِ ٱلرَّحۡمَٰنِ ٱلرَّحِيمِ

قُلۡ هُوَ ٱللَّهُ أَحَدٌ

Say:

He is Allah, the One and Only;

**Allah,**

**the Eternal, Absolute;**

He begets not, nor was He begotten;

وَلَمْ يَكُنْ لَّهُۥ كُفُوًا أَحَدٌ

**And there is none comparable unto Him.**

**Allah is beyond comparison. There is nothing comparable to Him in nature. There is none in the entire universe, who is equal to Allah. He is Unique in every aspect.**

www.ingramcontent.com/pod-product-compliance
Lightning Source LLC
Chambersburg PA
CBHW042115110726
48006CB00002B/649
*9798706747336*